Lagos: A Fun and Hectic City

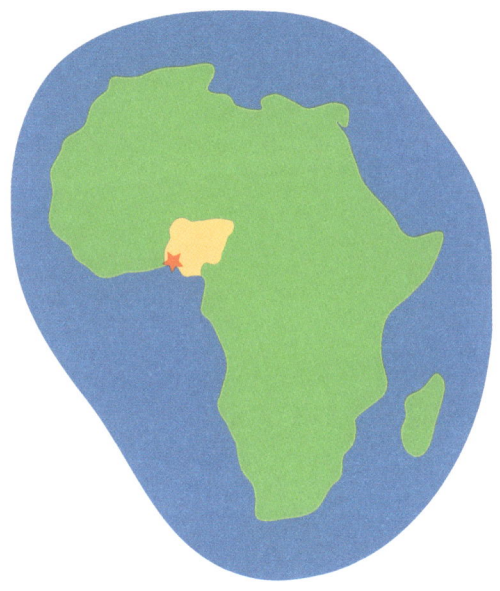

Chapter 4
Lesson 74: Spelling with -C
Lexile® Measure: 620L

ISBN 978-1-62382-033-6

Lagos is the biggest city in Nigeria. It is on the coast of the Atlantic Ocean in Africa. It is home to more than 15 million people. That is a lot of people! Some people say that Lagos will soon be the third-largest city in the world. With so many people, life in Lagos can be hectic. But it can also be fun.

Traffic in Lagos is very hectic. It can take three hours to drive 12 miles. In other cities, it takes only fifteen minutes to drive the same distance. That is a lot of traffic! Traffic jams are very common in Lagos. A traffic jam in this city could make you feel very frantic if you are in a rush.

Children in Lagos can attend school. They have an ethic of respect. They admire their teachers. They also admire people who are older than they are. Because of the hectic traffic, some students spend up to four hours a day on a school bus. When they get home, they are very tired.

People in Lagos like a wide range of ethnic music. They dance to hip-hop. They also dance to other kinds of music. Classic African-style drums are also used to make music. It is fun to see people play live music on the streets.

The climate in Lagos is hot and humid. There are two rainy seasons and two dry seasons. If you want to go on a picnic in Lagos, you will not want to go between April and July. It is very rainy at that time. When it is dry and hot, it is nice to go to one of the beaches.

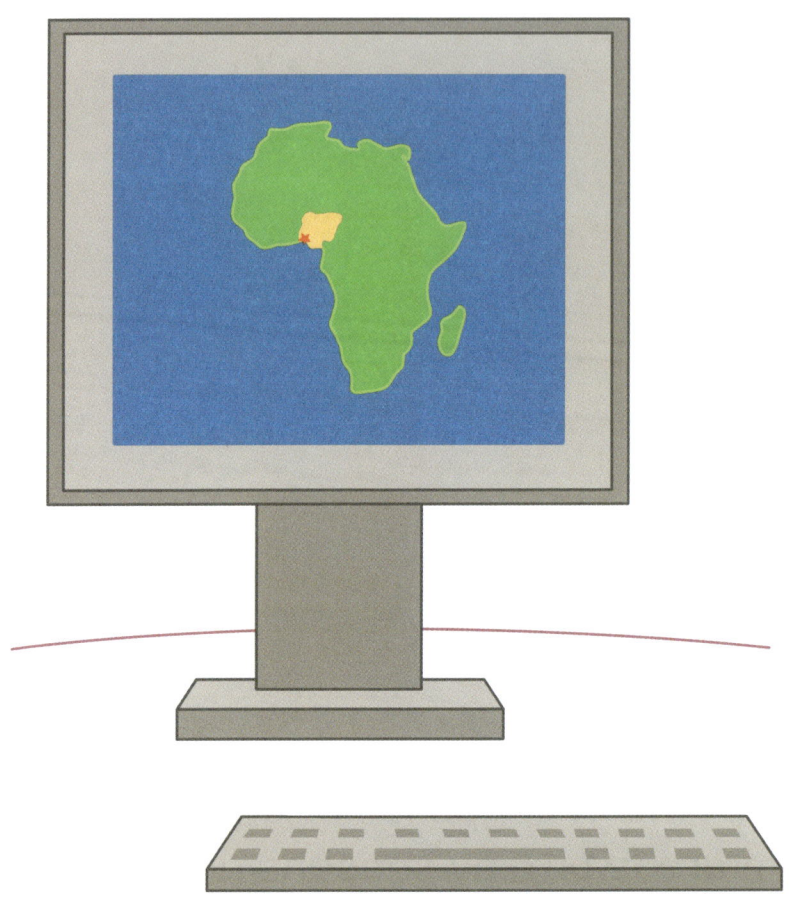

These are just some basic facts about Lagos. If you want to learn more, you can look it up on the Internet. Or, you can find a good book about this fun and hectic city.

The End

Comprehension Questions

1. What specific part of Africa is this passage about?

    a. a city

    b. a beach

    c. a country

2. How many people live in Lagos?

    a. 3 million

    b. 15 million

    c. 100 million

3. Which place is *hectic*?

    a. a library

    b. an empty bedroom

    c. a busy shopping center

4. If you have to be somewhere in Lagos at a certain time,

    a. it is best to leave very early.

    b. you can always get there quickly.

    c. make sure that you have a heavy coat.

5. Traffic in Lagos is very
    a. fast.

    b. hectic.

    c. smooth.

Skill Words

Atlantic	frantic	ethnic	basic
hectic	ethic	classic	
traffic	music	picnic	

Most Common Words

a	if	one	these
about	in	only	they
also	is	or	this
an	it	other	three
and	just	people	time
are	kinds	play	to
be	largest	same	two
because	learn	say	up
but	like	see	used
can	live	so	very
could	look	some	want
day	make	take	when
find	many	takes	who
get	more	than	will
go	not	that	with
good	of	the	world
have	older	their	you
home	on	there	

Challenge Words

Lagos	third	tired
city	hours	African
distance	cities	between
Nigeria	school	book
ocean	admire	
million	minutes	
soon	four	